D1014990

Food Risks
and Controversies

Food Risks and Controversies

MINIMIZING THE DANGERS IN YOUR DIET

BY CHARLES A. SALTER

THE MILLBROOK PRESS
BROOKFIELD, CONNECTICUT
A TEEN NUTRITION BOOK

I wish to acknowledge the support and assistance of
my editor at The Millbrook Press, Mr. Frank Menchaca.

Library of Congress Cataloging-in-Publication Data
Salter, Charles A., 1947–
Food risks and controversies : minimizing the dangers in your diet
by Charles A. Salter.
p.   cm.—(A Teen nutrition book)
Includes bibliographical references and index.
Summary: Introduces the health hazards associated with food,
examining such topics as manmade and natural toxins, food addi-
tives, and pesticides, and discusses how to eat safely and wisely.
ISBN 1-56294-259-X (lib. bdg.)
1. Food—Toxicology—Juvenile literature.   2. Nutritionally
induced diseases—Juvenile literature.   3. Diet in disease
—Juvenile literature.   [1. Food—Toxicology.   2. Nutrition.]
I. Title. II. Series.
RA1258.S35   1993
615.9'54—dc20   92-37442   CIP   AC

Published by The Millbrook Press
2 Old New Milford Road, Brookfield, Connecticut 06804

*This book is dedicated
to Dr. Matthew Herz,
a federal government manager
of food development research
who knows how to shed light
even in the midst of darkness.*

Contents

Food Risks
and Controversies

1

The Best of All Possible Worlds

You lie on the couch reading a comic book. You fall asleep and dream you become the superhero NUTRO-MIGHT!

Nothing stands in your way. You have the ability to right wrongs, defend the weak, and, most important, purify the world's food supply. With your cosmic force you can forever safeguard nutrition around the globe.

What will you do with your glorious new powers?

Of course, you'll fight to end crime, poverty, and war. But if you're like many teens today, you'll use your special powers over food to:

1. Zap all those fattening calories out of ice cream and the other rich treats you love.

2. Stop all snack manufacturers from using preservatives.
3. Restrict farmers from spraying crops with insecticides.
4. Inspire people to grow food organically.
5. Junk all those food chemicals that cause cancer.
6. Force manufacturers to tell the truth in their food ads and product labels.

Life in a
Risk-Free World

Wouldn't it be nice if you *were* NUTRO-MIGHT? Wouldn't it be great if we never had to worry about food making us sick? Imagine chomping into a juicy red apple without fretting that pesticides could turn it into a time bomb in our stomachs. We could live in a world without bugs to batter our crops, poisons to imperil our digestive systems, and toxins to terrify us. It would be the best of all possible worlds—a risk-free world.

Unfortunately, such a world doesn't exist. We are surrounded by risks, many of which come from the foods we depend upon to survive. People get poisoned, contract cancer, and die from the foods they eat. There are even disturbed individuals who deliberately put toxins such as cyanide in supermarket fruits and aspirin bottles.

Minimizing Risk

We can't avoid all food risks. But we can minimize them. In fact, some of our most brilliant minds have dedicated themselves to saving the agricultural environment, cutting fat, cholesterol, and calories from food, and reducing insects and fungi on food without adding dangerous poisons. Entire government agencies such as the U.S. Department of Agriculture and the U.S. Food and Drug Administration are devoted to screening our food supply to make it as safe as possible.

Despite the problems we now face, we have come a long way over the centuries. In the Middle Ages grain crops sometimes grew moldy with a fungus called ergot. Not knowing the dangers of ergot, people sometimes ate the infected rye or wheat.

The results were incredible. Ergot produces effects similar to those of the illegal drug LSD. Eating it causes the disorder known as ergotism, sometimes called "Saint Anthony's fire." The symptoms include hallucinations (perceiving things that aren't there), delusions (believing things that aren't true), and bizarre behavior. Severe ergotism reduces the blood flow to the arms and legs, sometimes causing tissue death or gangrene and even loss of a limb. Imagine how a teen felt a few centuries ago if she merely ate a slice of bread and suddenly found herself going crazy!

Luckily, Americans don't have similar outbreaks of ergotism these days because scientists discovered the cause and how to prevent it. Knowledgeable farmers and federal inspectors now screen crops to make sure that no infected produce reaches the marketplace.

Ergot is just one food risk that scientists and food producers have controlled. But others remain to be conquered. New strains of infectious bacteria and viruses continue to develop. Government, scientists, and homemakers can all work together to understand, control, and minimize food risks. In addition, there are things teens can do every day to lessen their health risks from food.

How Do You Perceive Risk?

You can start by establishing your current attitudes toward food risks. Please answer the following questions based on your opinions right now. No one expects you to know all the correct answers to these questions yet. The correct answers follow, and these may help you realize how many misconceptions about food exist today.

1. Which type of food chemical most frequently poses a risk to human health?

a. Artificial chemicals for food preservation, coloring, or flavor.
b. Natural chemicals that develop in fruits and vegetables as they grow.

2. Which type of food chemical poses the most serious risk?

   a. Molds and other fungi that grow on foods naturally.
   b. Artificial chemicals added to food to kill fungi.

3. Large doses of certain artificial sweeteners like saccharin can cause tumors in rats, though there is some dispute over whether these are cancerous. What is the risk to humans of consuming moderate amounts of saccharin over a lifetime?

   a. Approximately twice that of peanut butter.
   b. About half that of one fresh mushroom.
   c. About one percent that of wine.
   d. All of the above.

4. About how many deaths in the United States are caused each year by foodborne

(a term meaning derived from food) ill-nesses or diseases?

    a. 900
    b. 9,000
    c. 90,000
    d. 900,000

5. Which of the following diseases may be spread through eating contaminated food?

    a. Infectious hepatitis (a liver dis-ease).
    b. Amoebic dysentery (which causes severe diarrhea).
    c. Tapeworm infestation.
    d. All of the above.
    e. None of the above.

6. Many Japanese eat a raw fish which if prepared correctly is safe and delicious but if prepared improperly can be fatally poisonous.

    a. True
    b. False

7. Foodborne diseases can best be pre-vented by:

    a. Buying only organically grown

foods (those without pesticides or
artificial fertilizers).

b. Avoiding all restaurant foods.
c. Proper food handling and storage
at home.
d. Avoiding all canned foods.

Answers

Now let's see the accuracy of your opinions on food
risks.

1. The correct answer is *b.* Some artificial
chemicals used in food production do
carry some risk, but chemicals with a major potential for danger are banned by the
federal government. A wide variety of
chemicals growing naturally in certain
foods can cause cancer, genetic mutations, and other problems. Luckily, any
given food contains only small quantities
of each of these chemicals. But a tiny risk
still exists. We'll explore this in Chapter 3.

2. *a.* Most fungicides (fungus-killing substances) and other chemicals sprayed on
food pose only a small risk at worst, because little if any survives by the time you

eat the food. Some molds (but not all) that grow naturally on exposed food, however, are deadly. Certain molds on peanuts or corn, for example, produce aflatoxin. Even tiny amounts can cause liver cancer, genetic mutations, and immune system problems. Fortunately, the federal government limits the amount of such molds allowed to enter the food supply. We'll explore this in Chapter 3.

3. *d*. Of all the foods mentioned in this question, the only two that receive much bad press are wine and saccharin. Wine receives bad press because it is alcohol. The government sought to ban saccharin in 1972 after some studies showed it could increase the risk of contracting cancer. However, the public demanded that saccharin remain on the market. And, in terms of risk magnitude, this seems sensible. Saccharin poses a smaller risk than many other food ingredients that are widely accepted. Chapter 2 explains more about artificial sweeteners.

4. *b*. Though some risks, such as that from saccharin, have been greatly exaggerated, don't conclude that food carries no risk. As recently as 1988 in the United

States, 9,000 people died from foodborne diseases. And millions of others contracted non-fatal, but still unpleasant illnesses. Common food poisoning usually consists of about three days of cramps, diarrhea, and vomiting. This is the subject of Chapter 6.

5. *d.* Contaminated food can spread all of these—and many other—diseases. That does not mean, however, that bad food is the only cause of these illnesses. Chapter 6 examines this topic.

6. *True!* To make this fish, called *fugu*, safe, chefs must carefully remove poison sacs from the fish. Every year chefs goof, and some diners die. The fact that many people are willing to play "Russian roulette" with food shows how people differ on perception of risk and willingness to take risk. I wouldn't chance it, but many do. Would you?

7. *c.* Many people are more concerned about their sources of food than how they handle food once they've bought it. But poor food handling and storage causes most foodborne disease problems. In fact, even if you buy contaminated food,

proper handling can often remove the danger. Chapter 6 shows you how.

Some of these answers probably surprised you. They could even have surprised NUTRO-MIGHT. They demonstrate, however, how much there is to discover about food risks.

2

Fake Fat and
Simulated Sugar:
*Artificial Foods
in the Diet*

"Have your cake and eat it, too." Is any promise more dazzling? Wouldn't it be great to eat cake, ice cream, cookies, candy, and pie without anxiety over the calories?

For years we've had artificial sweeteners that slashed most of the calories from soda and other soft drinks. Others are on the way. Fake fats have been developed that can reduce the fat-calories in ice cream and cake as well. But are these compounds safe? And do they really reduce total caloric intake?

Artificial
Sweeteners

People have valued sugar for its sweet taste for thousands of years. In biblical times, honey was highly prized for providing a sweet flavor and energy. By 400 B.C. sugarcane was used as a sweetener in India. For centuries people have known how to refine sugar—that is, to separate it from plant foods containing it such as sugarcane and sugar beets.

Today, sugar serves as a major ingredient in candy, cakes, and most other desserts. It is also present in an incredible variety of processed foods—items ranging from breakfast cereals to lasagna. It is even used as a food preservative. The average person each year consumes over 100 pounds of it. Many people eat their weight in sugar each year!

There are many types of real sugar. Sucrose, called "table sugar," is the form most often purchased and used by consumers. Each molecule of sucrose consists of a molecule of glucose, also called dextrose, and one of fructose. Fructose, sometimes called "fruit sugar," exists in a wide variety of fruits and berries. Another sugar, lactose, occurs naturally in milk. These and other substances with names ending in "-ose" are naturally occurring sugars.

Scientists years ago discovered, however, that real sugar had drawbacks. It contains calories (16 per teaspoonful), thus adding to the average waistline, and contributes heavily to tooth decay. Since it is cheap, plentiful, and tasty, people consume more and more of it. So the search began for artificial sweeteners that would provide the flavor of sugar without rotting the teeth or swelling the waistline.

Types of
Artificial Sweeteners

So far that search has yielded mixed results. The artificial sweeteners we use today all have fewer calories than sugar, while comparison testing reveals that they taste far sweeter than sugar. But they have drawbacks not found in sugar. They appear below in order of increasing potency.

• *Cyclamate.* This artificial sweetener is 30 times as sweet as table sugar, but was banned by the U.S. Food and Drug Administration (FDA) in 1970 after several studies linked it to cancer. Interestingly, Canadian authorities, examining the same scientific evidence, declared the risk so small that they allowed cyclamates in their food supply. In fact, some 50 countries around the world allow cyclamates, and the FDA is reconsidering the issue. Perhaps the United States will again allow this sweetener to be used.

• *Aspartame (NutraSweet).* This sweetener was first discovered in 1965 but not approved by the FDA for commercial use until 1981, after years of exhaustive testing. It is composed not of sugar but of protein. Two amino acids, components of protein, called aspartic acid and phenylalanine are bound together in each molecule of aspartame. It is digested normally like other proteins and contains one or two calories per serving as a result. Aspartame is about 180 times sweeter than sucrose. However, heating can break up the molecule and destroy its sweetness. If you leave a can of aspartame-sweetened soda in the sun or a warm room for several days it may lose much of its sweetness, though it is still safe to drink.

• *Acesulfame-K (Sunette)*. This compound is 200 times as sweet as table sugar and has been approved for food use by the FDA. It contains no calories because it cannot be metabolized or chemically broken down by the body. Therefore, it passes out of the body unchanged in the waste. Heat doesn't destroy acesulfame-K, so it can be used in cooking.

• *Saccharin*. This synthetic compound contains no calories yet tastes about 300 to 500 times sweeter than table sugar. It takes only a tiny bit to sweeten a soft drink or cup of coffee. Used in food since the early 1900s, saccharin was considered safe and appeared on the U.S. government's first GRAS (generally recognized as safe) list of food ingredients in 1959. However, it was removed from that list in 1972, and further studies over the years have confirmed that it can increase one's chances of getting cancer. But when the FDA sought to ban saccharin, it met with a widespread public uproar and backed off the ban. Today, the potential value of the sweetener to reduce caloric intake and tooth decay is generally considered to outweigh the small cancer risk of moderate use.

• *Sucralose.* This compound also contains no calories yet tastes 600 times as sweet as sugar. The FDA, however, has not yet approved it. It will require years of successful testing before the FDA considers it proven safe enough for commercial use.

• *Alitame.* This is another experimental sweetener that has not yet been approved by the FDA for use in food. At 2,000 times the sweetness of sugar, it possesses incredible potency. A tiny grain of it provides the same sweetness as an entire teaspoon of sugar. It is also more stable than many sweeteners, not breaking down in heat as aspartame does. If it survives all safety testing and gains approval by the FDA, it could become a leading sweetener.

Risks and Limitations of Artificial Sweeteners

Despite the apparent potential for cutting calories, unrestricted use of artificial sugars is not recommended.

• *They may stimulate rather than reduce appetite.* Artificial sweeteners are supposed to replace high-calorie sugar with compounds containing few or

TABLE 2.1
AVERAGE USE OF SWEETENERS
PER PERSON

Type	Use in 1975	Use in 1987
Real Sugars	118 pounds	133 pounds
Artificial Sweeteners	6 pounds	19 pounds

no calories. Theoretically, one's total intake of calories and body weight should decline as a result. But studies show that while we consume more of these sugar alternatives we also consume more real sugar and the incidence of obesity increases. Counting the use in food processing, our annual use of both real and artificial sugars has risen steadily. (See Table 2.1.)

It appears that we are becoming addicted to sweet tastes and want them more and more. Some research suggests that the extreme sweetness of artificial sugars may actually stimulate appetite and cause us to eat more of all foods.

• *Some people may be sensitive or allergic to certain artificial sweeteners.* About 1 in 10,000 children is born without the ability to metabolize phenylalanine, a common component of aspartame or NutraSweet, which doesn't bother most people. In these kids, toxic levels of phenylalanine by-products can build up and damage the brain, causing hyperactivity, retardation, or convulsions. The only solution involves minimizing phenylalanine intake, which means minimizing aspartame, but parents won't do this unless they know about the problem. A simple blood test at birth can detect this condition, known as PKU, or phenylketonuria.

• *No artificial sweeteners behave in food quite like sugar.* A tiny bit of aspartame can produce the sweet taste of sugar. But it won't add the bulk and texture of real sugar needed to make a cake. And while sugar melts during cooking to enrich flavor, aspartame breaks down at high temperatures and loses its sweetness. Not all uses of sugar, therefore, can be replaced with artificial sweeteners.

• *Safety testing usually assumes certain intake levels, above which the effects are less well known.* Originally, aspartame was used in only a few foods, and overall intakes were low. At daily consumption levels below 50 milligrams per kilogram of body weight, the compound was certified to be safe. (This works out to a maximum of about 15 cans of aspartame-sweetened soda per day for a 130-pound teen.) But its increasing popularity has led to its inclusion in more and more foods, and average intakes now exceed those that were originally expected. Some teens who consume many different aspartame-sweetened products may actually exceed the recommended intake limit. Hundreds of people have complained to the federal government about headaches and other vague symptoms from high doses of aspartame. It is still generally considered safe for all but those with phenylketonuria. But the long-term effects in humans of extremely high intake levels are simply not known.

These represent the positive and negative aspects of sugar and sugar substitutes. But what about another substance that is present in a wide variety of foods we eat—fat?

Food Fats

Fat occurs not only as streaks in meat. It is also present in oils, vegetables, nuts, and snacks or in the cream in dairy products. Fat adds flavor and body to food, but too much can also add weight to your body. Real fats constitute our most concentrated source of food energy. An ounce of pure fat (the amount in about six teaspoons of butter or margarine, in three and one-half cups of whole milk, or in a quarter-pound hamburger) contains 255 calories. This is more than twice the energy of pure protein or carbohydrate, each of which has 114 calories per ounce. Animal fats, found in meat and dairy products, also have cholesterol and saturated fat, an excess of which contributes to heart disease. In our society, the average teen consumes far more calories and cholesterol than desirable. What if we could keep the flavor and texture of food fat but cut down the calories?

Artificial Fats

Artificial fats contain no cholesterol and have far fewer calories than natural food fats. Yet they have approximately the same flavor and texture as the real thing. Here are some of the types available now or soon to come out on the market:

• *Simplesse.* The NutraSweet Company, the same organization that gave us one of our most popular artificial sweeteners, developed Simplesse from blending egg white and casein (milk protein) together at high speed. Simplesse's first commercial use has been in frozen desserts intended to replace ice cream. While a four-ounce serving of ice cream may contain about 15 grams of fat and 250 calories, the same size serving of Simple Pleasures with Simplesse has only one gram of fat and about 120 calories. Does it taste the same? Try it for yourself and see. The drawback to Simplesse is that heat makes it tough and unusable. Therefore, it can't be used to replace the fat in cooked foods. It will no doubt be added to a number of other foods such as dairy products and salad dressings.

• *Olestra.* Procter & Gamble developed this artificial fat. Unlike Simplesse, Olestra can be used in cooked foods. Its original name was sucrose poly-ester, because it is composed of sucrose and fatty acids, both of which are normal, digestible food ingredients. However, the human body cannot break down the chemical connections between these ingredients in Olestra. Thus Olestra, when consumed, remains indigestible and adds no calories to your body. In this respect, Olestra resembles food fiber, which passes out of the body as solid waste. The FDA has not yet approved it for food use, however.

• *Stellar.* The A.E. Staley Company produced this whipped blend of corn starch and water. Like Simplesse, Stellar consists of all-natural ingredients and is fully digestible. But it contains only about one-tenth the calories of real fat and no cholesterol at all. Unlike Simplesse, it can be used in most heated products, such as cakes and soups. However, certain forms of cooking such as frying do break it down. This excludes it from use in deep-fat fryers with such foods as chicken or french fries. Stellar has not yet received FDA approval.

Possible Risks of Artificial Fats

The Food and Drug Administration has conducted studies showing that Simplesse is safe. However, the FDA conducts little testing of new products such as Simplesse and Stellar that are composed of natural food ingredients already known to be safe. The FDA focuses its testing predominantly on new artificial compounds such as Olestra. The FDA won't approve a new chemical for use in food until years of safety testing have proven that it doesn't cause cancer, genetic mutations, or other health problems.

However, there may be other risks to artificial fats:

• *Some teens may be allergic to the ingredients used in artificial fats.* Simplesse contains milk protein, and Stellar has corn carbohydrate. If you are allergic to either of those ingredients, you would want to avoid the respective compound containing it. Proper labeling of food products should help reduce that risk.

• *Fat substitutes may not aid weight loss or maintenance.* At first glance, this seems impossible. Reducing calories through eating less or exercising more definitely helps you lose weight. But if you consume large amounts of products containing lower calorie fake fats, you still may not reduce your total caloric intake or lose weight. Knowing that your frozen dessert contains half the calories of ice cream, you may simply be tempted to eat twice as much. Because of the allure of rich desserts and snacks, your eating habits may grow worse instead of better.

• *The effects of long-term, heavy use are not clear.*
Consuming a substance occasionally and in small
quantities may not upset your system. But what if
you eat that substance in large quantities for years?
If the FDA could foresee terrible risks in that, it
would limit or ban the product. So the risk may be
only slight, but how slight? We won't know the
effects of heavy use of fake fat products for many
years. Until then, you might try these products,
but avoid becoming "hooked" on them.

Low Calorie
Artificial Foods

It was a dramatic day on the television talk show
hosted by Oprah Winfrey in 1988 when Oprah an-
nounced that she had lost 67 pounds using a liquid
diet product. Her delight shone as she bragged
about wearing her old jeans again for the first time
in years. Oprah electrified the viewing public. At
last, it seemed to many, an answer to their own
desperate craving to lose weight! The company that
made the product soon received a million calls from
eager would-be dieters as a result.

The product is just one of the many diet plans
that depend on artificial foods to control caloric
intake. Such programs teach that people gain
weight from eating normal foods, but they can lose

weight by depending upon scientifically crafted meal replacements low in calories.

These liquid foods do play an important role in the world of nutrition. Injured or sick people with broken jaws or diseases of the digestive tract, for example, can't eat normal food. They must rely on artificial, liquid foods until they get better. But should the average, healthy person concerned with body weight depend on such products? Probably not, for several reasons:

• *Weight lost by using artificial foods usually returns.* Oprah Winfrey, for example, regained all of her lost weight within two years. Her weight loss gave liquid diets immeasurable free publicity, but her subsequent regain cast them all in a bad light. And her experience is all too typical. Studies reveal that the majority of liquid diet users soon regain at least half the weight lost. Many regain all they lost plus a "kicker" of a few extra pounds.

• *Artificial foods leave out not only many calories but also several other nutrients.* Scientists continually discover new nutrients or new information about how much of certain nutrients we need. Until our knowledge of nutrition is complete, foods developed artificially will always be inferior to natural, whole foods. Even products that include extra amounts of certain nutrients will leave others out. Liquid diets, for instance, contain little fiber, the lack of which may lead to constipation. Furthermore, many lack important trace minerals (those needed in only small amounts—for example, iron, zinc, and fluoride).

• *Some liquid diets are dangerous.* Some early liquid diets were so unbalanced nutritionally that dozens of users actually died. Don't rely even on the most balanced of modern versions, excluding real food, unless under the supervision of a physician, who can catch ill effects early.

• *Reliance on artificial foods teaches nothing about normal eating.* Artificial foods become a crutch for some people. When forsaking all their favorite treats, they do lose weight. But as soon as they leave the protein powders and drinks behind, they fall back into their old eating habits. They then regain all the weight they lost. They have not learned how to select, prepare, and eat normal foods wisely.

What You Can Do

• Avoid excess of both real and artificial sweeteners. Not every food and beverage must taste sweet. Some authorities recommend intake limits of no more than three to four packets of Equal (powdered aspartame) or three to four servings of aspartame-sweetened foods and beverages per day. This is even more conservative than the FDA's maximum limit. Avoid completely any sweetener to which you may be allergic. Without medical testing you may not be sure about allergies, but listen to your body. If you note a headache, difficulty in breathing, or other unpleasant symptoms every time you consume a certain compound, give it up. If your symptoms subside, try living without that compound. Take serious or worrisome problems to your physician.

• Try the artificial fat foods if you wish, but don't use them as a crutch. In addition, don't use the calories you save as an excuse to eat more high-fat treats.

• Unless prescribed by a physician, don't rely on protein drinks and other artificial foods as a replacement for normal meals. No edibles designed by a food manufacturer can ever be as healthy for you in the long run as a normal, well-balanced diet of regular whole foods.

3

Food Additives:
Adding or Subtracting
Food Safety?

Food additives have a checkered past. Would you knowingly:

1. Put toxic lead or arsenic compounds in candy to give it brighter colors?
2. Add grated charcoal to black pepper to increase its weight for sale?
3. Process food using filthy equipment and store it in an environment filled with rodents and insects?

Of course not. Yet these and many other dangerous practices have occurred in the food industry in the past. For this reason, the government had to step in.

Federal
Safety Controls

During the 1700s America had no national regulations to prevent unscrupulous or ignorant food manufacturers from introducing contaminants into the food supply. A few statutes or laws in colonial times protected the purity of bread and meat. But not until 1886 did Congress intervene in a major food-purity issue. Based on our understanding today, however, we would conclude it took the wrong side. At issue was whether oleomargarine, a type of artificial butter developed in France, should be allowed into the American food supply. American dairy farmers lobbied against it, fearing competition with the real butter they produced. Congress sided with the dairy lobby, taxing and restricting margarine nationally until 1950, though not banning it outright. Now, however, we realize that margarine's lack of animal fat and cholesterol, present in butter, are health advantages.

In the twenty years after 1886, the "pure food" movement grew and crusaded increasingly for federal laws to protect the nation's food supply. Finally, in 1906, Congress passed the first Food and Drug Act, and President Theodore Roosevelt, who had long favored such an act, happily signed it into law.

In 1927 the Food, Drug, and Insecticide Administration was formed. This was the forerunner of the Food and Drug Administration (FDA) of today. In its early days, however, this organization had to prove that a food additive was dangerous before it could be banned. This meant that potentially hazardous compounds could be introduced into the nation's food supply without any prior safety testing. Only when actual health problems developed could the product be removed from the market.

The Federal Food, Drug, and Cosmetic Act of 1938 became law and extended the government's power. This act closed some of the loopholes in the 1906 law. The earlier law allowed, for example, a manufacturer who gave a "distinctive name" to a product to include whatever the producer wanted in it. For example, a generic product such as "bread" had to be pure, but a bread-like product called "vita-toast" could include anything. The 1938 act, however, eliminated such exceptions. This act also provided for much stiffer penalties for pure-food violations than did the earlier version, with fines up to $10,000 and imprisonment up to three years for repeat offenses. The 1938 act remains the foundation upon which our food-safety laws rest.

It has been updated and strengthened many times since. For example, the Food Additives

Amendment of 1958 required prior testing of compounds intended for use in food. A food manufacturer had to prove that an ingredient was safe first rather than use it until the FDA could prove it dangerous.

To enforce its rulings today, the FDA has not only a national headquarters but also 6 regional offices, 22 district offices, and nearly 150 resident posts of inspectors around the country.

Additive
Approval Criteria

The laws discussed in the previous section make it very difficult for a manufacturer to introduce any new chemical into the food supply. Each new food additive must undergo years of expensive and thorough scientific testing on at least two different species of animals. The FDA then decides whether the additive appears to be safe and effective. There are three main criteria the FDA is concerned with:

1. *Detectability*—Can the additive still be measured in the final food product? (Some break down chemically.)
2. *Effectiveness*—Does the additive do what it is supposed to do? (If not, why add it?)
3. *Safety*—When fed in large doses to ani-

mals in controlled studies, does the additive cause genetic mutations, cancer, or other diseases?

If a compound meets all three criteria, it is usually approved. But approval is not necessarily permanent. If further research raises additional health concerns, the FDA can rethink the matter at any time and ban the compound if it sees fit.

Allowable Levels

In most cases, additive safety need not be absolute. Most chemicals are safe in low doses, and most can be dangerous in excess. Food additives and contaminants are usually expressed as a proportion of the total matter present in a food— either in parts per million (ppm), per billion (ppb), or per trillion (ppt). The more sensitive our food-testing methods, the more contaminants we can detect, even those at levels with no practical health significance. Yet the more chemicals that can be detected in food, the more the fear of possible contamination.

Tests on animals are designed to determine the maximum proportion of additives in a product without causing any noticeable health problems. As a further margin of safety, the amount allowable in human food is set as 1 percent of that strength level. For instance, if 1,050 ppm of Compound X causes disease in rats, but 1,000 ppm shows no ill effects, then the maximum allowed in human food is 10 ppm (1 percent of 1,000 = 10).

The Delaney Clause

A key portion of the Food Additives Amendment of 1958 was dubbed the Delaney Clause, in honor of the congressman who chaired the hearings on food chemicals and safety. The Delaney Clause states that "no additive shall be deemed safe if it is found to induce cancer when ingested by man or animal. . . ."

The Delaney Clause has often been criticized as being too strict. It allows no risk in the case of food additives linked to cancer. Yet many cancer-causing compounds occur in foods naturally and are not banned. Aflatoxin, for instance, grows naturally in moldy peanuts, and it is fifty million times more potent than saccharin in causing cancer. The government cannot simply ban it, for no one puts it there deliberately. The FDA, however, does regulate how much of it reaches the food marketplace. Inspectors test batches of peanuts, and if one batch shows aflatoxin over the limit of 20 ppb, it cannot be sold as is. Rather than destroy the bad batch, however, the food company will often dilute it with a purer batch so that the average aflatoxin level in the combined batch falls below the limit. This may sound objectionable, but it is legal under the current system. Should the government allow levels of natural toxins that are far more dangerous than levels of artificial additives currently in use?

To get around the absolute ban of the Delaney Clause, the FDA is trying to implement a *de minimis non curat lex* policy. This Latin term means that the law should not concern itself with minimal food threats when there are other, more serious threats. The problem is: how to determine what is minimal? The FDA would like the freedom to ignore weak additives and contaminants that only increase the chances of getting cancer by less than one in a million.

This policy is very controversial. Certainly if you were that one person in a million who got cancer from a food deemed minimally threatening, you would be upset with the policy. But the FDA, like any other human institution, has limited personnel and financial resources. Some experts think that it makes sense to focus only on the threats to public health far greater than one in a million. It is estimated, for example, that the total risk of all food additives combined causes only about 1 percent of cancer deaths, while tobacco use alone causes 30 percent and diet causes 35 percent. (Most of these dietary deaths are caused by consuming excess fat and cholesterol and insufficient fiber).

What do you think? Should the FDA struggle to cope with all risks, great and small, or dedicate itself to fighting only the larger risks?

Generally Recognized as Safe (GRAS) Additives

When the Food Additives Amendment became law in 1958, several hundred compounds were exempted from the need for specific testing. If decades of commercial use presented no serious or widespread health problems, the compound was presumed safe. This allowed the FDA to focus on new compounds about which little was known.

TABLE 3.1
SOME GENERALLY RECOGNIZED
AS SAFE (GRAS) ADDITIVES

Salt

Sugar

Vitamins and minerals

Carob bean gum, pectin,
and other food texturizers

Proprionic acid, sodium benzoate,
and other food preservatives

Vanilla, herbs,
and other natural flavorings

The first GRAS list held over 200 compounds, but it now has about 700. Some of the more common compounds appear in Table 3.1. But because an item is included in the GRAS list does not mean it always stays there. Though additional testing is not required by law, new research methods continue to shed further light on some additives. If new data indicate a hazard from a GRAS item, as occurred with cyclamates, the FDA can rethink the issue and even ban the chemical.

Types of
Food Additives

The Food and Drug Administration has approved more than 2,800 different food additives. Most fall under a handful of categories. See Table 3.2.

• *Coloring Agents.* Many compounds, including Blue #1, Red #3, and Yellow #5, are added to foods simply to improve their color and appearance. Many candies and beverages would have a dull or bland appearance if not for colorants. Imagine how M&M's would seem if they were only produced in a dull brown.

• *Flavoring Agents and Enhancers.* Some compounds such as spices and sugar add new flavors to food. Other compounds such as salt and monosodium glutamate enhance the flavors already present in food.

TABLE 3.2
CATEGORIES OF FOOD ADDITIVES

Colors
Flavors
Nutrients
Preservatives
Texturizers

• *Nutrient Supplementation.* Many foods are fortified with added nutrients, sometimes to eradicate previously widespread nutritional deficiency diseases. For instance, vitamin D is put in milk to help prevent rickets, iodine in salt to preclude goiter, and vitamin B_1 in bread to avoid beriberi. At other times, nutrients are added simply to increase sales appeal. For instance, many breakfast cereals include unnecessary vitamin surpluses.

• *Preservatives.* Prepared foods won't last long if exposed to the environment. Untreated bread, for instance, will grow hard and stale within hours of being left open on the kitchen counter. Within a day or two it will grow moldy and become completely inedible. Storage in closed containers or refrigeration delays spoilage. But many chemicals are added to food to help resist deterioration. Such chemicals include antioxidants (for example, BHT, or butylated hydroxytoluene) to slow the chemical breakdown of food molecules by oxygen. Also, antibacterial and antifungal agents (for example, potassium sorbate or sodium nitrite) help to delay the growth of microorganisms and molds in food.

• *Texturizers.* Some additives are used to improve the texture or consistency of food products. For example, texturizers help bread and other baked products retain their moisture, and they prevent caking or clumping in powdered foods. Many ice creams and other dairy products contain the texturizer carrageenan. This compound serves as an emulsifier, which helps in mixing together different liquids such as cream and milk. Carrageenan also helps to thicken ice cream and keep the ingredients from separating out during storage. This additive makes ice cream more enjoyable, but did you know it comes from seaweed? A name such as carrageenan on an ingredients label sounds technical, important, and reassuring, whereas a name such as "seaweed extract" might turn customers off. Yet that is exactly what carrageenan is.

Are Food Additives Dangerous?

The general public sometimes reacts with alarm at the hundreds of additives in our food supply. When you see a name such as BHA (butylated hydroxyanisole) on a food label, does it turn your stomach? Do you feel that you wandered into a chemistry lab rather than a food store?

Actually, such chemicals pose far less danger than some might believe:

• As soon as scientific studies prove any additive to be dangerous, it is usually banned. Public outcry for the product, as in the case of saccharin, may, however, reverse the ban.

• Some food ingredients, including both natural and artificial additives, may be dangerous in large quantities, but they are quite safe in the limited doses typically encountered by teens. For instance, drinking one soft drink containing saccharin per day almost certainly wouldn't affect you, while consuming your annual dose all at once would. But other than in controlled scientific studies, no one would consume such megadoses. You wouldn't drink 365 cans of soda in one day.

• We must consider the relative benefit as well as the risk of food additives. In every case of approved additives, the estimated benefit exceeds the risk. For instance, consuming rancid or bad fat in snacks would be more harmful than eating the tiny bit of preservatives they contain to prevent fat rancidity. Some experts even argue that such chemicals may actually benefit the human body.

• Just because an additive is a "chemical" doesn't make it suspicious. All foods consist of chemicals, whether natural or artificial. Your body can't distinguish between vitamins grown in food naturally or later added artificially. Sodium chloride (table salt) is still sodium chloride whether it's found in seawater, mined naturally from the ground, or created artificially in the laboratory. But to some teens "sodium chloride" on a food label looks scarier than "salt." It's all a matter of familiar terms versus technical ones.

Salt—The Number One Additive

In fact, the most common food additive—ordinary salt—may be one of the most dangerous, and yet few teens think anything of it. Many foods contain salt naturally. The food industry adds it to almost every processed food, such as lunchmeats, frozen dinners, and canned pasta, because salt enhances flavor and helps preserve food. Many homemakers freely pour it when cooking, and many consumers also liberally sprinkle it when dining. By the time that first forkful of food hits your taste buds, it may be steeped in salt.

Our bodies require small amounts of salt. Without it we would die, for the two ions in salt—sodium and chloride—help the nerves work and maintain the fluid balance in living cells. But many experts estimate that teens now consume twenty to thirty times their salt requirements.

Excess salt consumption over a long period may increase the risk of high blood pressure, at least in people with a genetic predisposition to this problem. And elevated blood pressure over time can lead to strokes, heart attacks, and other deadly circulatory system problems. Too much salt all at once can lead to poisoning, though this is rare and won't occur with ordinary foods.

Individual Differences in Sensitivity to Additives

Salt illustrates a problem that complicates the issue of the safety of food additives. Some people can tolerate a given additive dose with no harmful effect, while others consuming the same dose may become violently ill. Some teens are *sensitive* to a given compound: they react at a dose level lower than most people. Other teens are *allergic*: their systems react in an abnormal way, which others wouldn't experience even at much higher doses.

True allergies occur when one's immune system mobilizes against a food protein or other large molecule as if it were an invading disease organism. The system produces antibodies to attack the molecules and causes reactions such as nausea, rashes, swelling, and difficulty in breathing. Some teens are allergic to certain whole foods, such as milk, eggs, nuts, or strawberries. Others are allergic to specific food additives. Some teens have a *food intolerance*, which is an unpleasant bodily reaction in the absence of an immune response.

Key Additives That Affect Only Some Teens

The following food additives may cause reactions in you.

• *MSG (Monosodium Glutamate)*. Your NUTRO-MIGHT hotline rings. A woman sounding scared explains that she loves Chinese food, but dining in her favorite restaurant the last few times she has become ill—as she is now. You inquire about the symptoms. She reports a terrible headache, facial flushing, and a hot burning sensation throughout the skin. She declares that someone is trying to poison her and pleads for your help.

You fly to her side at the Golden Dragon, where she sits red-faced, bent over in pain, beside a steaming plate of egg *foo yong*. Is this the dish that's made you sick before, you ask, thinking the eggs could be tainted. No, she says, last time it was *kung pao* pork; before that it was *moo goo gai pan*.

You check out the kitchen. Everything seems sanitary and safe. The chef looks worried but innocent. Are you putting anything new or different in the food, you ask. He shakes his head. You stand and watch while he prepares several dishes. Then it hits you—the common ingredient in almost all of the dishes is monosodium glutamate, or MSG. You know it is used widely to enhance flavor. You remember that it has been blamed for the "Chinese restaurant syndrome," which afflicts one out of several hundred diners. (Some think this may be a true allergy, while others think it is mainly psychological.)

You return to the table, to see your client looking much improved already. I've solved the mystery, you say. You can enjoy all the Chinese food you want, but ask the chef to skip the MSG.

She smiles in relief. Thank you, NUTRO-MIGHT!

• *Sulfites.* These are types of salt that contain sulfur, and they are used widely to preserve food. In fact, sulfites were originally on the GRAS list. Dried fruits such as apricots often contain so much that you can smell the sulfur. Sulfites are also used in many processed foods, drugs, and alcoholic beverages, particularly wines. Sulfites once were used on raw fruits and vegetables at salad bars, but they were banned in 1986 because several cases of severe asthma, even deaths, were traced to their use. In 1987 the FDA decided to require mandatory warning labels on all foods containing more than 10 ppm of sulfites. Not everyone is sensitive to sulfites, but an estimated one million Americans are. The problem is that labels won't help people who aren't aware that they're sensitive to sulfites. Furthermore, some people may be sensitive even at doses under 10 ppm, which are not labeled. If you fit into this hypersensitive group, watch out for foods with these ingredients: potassium bisulfite, potassium metabisulfite, sodium bisulfite, sodium metabisulfite, and sulfur dioxide. If eating such foods gives you difficulty breathing, itchy rashes, or other pronounced symptoms, then avoid them.

• *Lactose Intolerance.* Lactose is a type of sugar that occurs naturally in all milk products. It adds taste and provides energy, and causes no problems for most people. However, some people produce an insufficient supply of the enzyme lactase, which is required to digest lactose. If they eat normal milk products, the undigested lactose reaches their intestines. There it attracts water, causing swelling and discomfort. The bacteria that are normally in the intestines use it to produce acid and gas, causing additional cramping, nausea, and diarrhea, usually within one-half to one hour after eating. Lactose intolerance is not uncommon among teens and increases with age. Therefore, just because you can tolerate lactose now does not mean you always will. If you have the problem, you have two choices:

One: Avoid normal milk products and foods or drugs to which lactose has been added in processing. If you choose this option, be sure to get calcium from other sources since milk is normally the best one. You may be able to tolerate fermented milk products such as yogurt, sour cream, and cultured buttermilk, as well as other products where milk is an ingredient but has been altered significantly. Non-milk foods rich in calcium include sardines, shrimp, other seafood, spinach, broccoli, other green leafy vegetables, soybeans, tofu, and nuts.

Two: You can consume milk and milk products if you add the enzyme lactase at the same time. You can buy lactase in liquid or tablet form over-the-counter. You can swallow these tablets with your food or dissolve them in a liquid to put directly into food.

• *Hyperactivity and the Feingold Diet.* Hyperactive children are those with short attention spans who seem unable to control their impulses and activity. They dart about, getting into mischief and generally causing disorder. Parents often try to strictly discipline hyperactive children but such measures often do not seem to work. Certain prescribed drugs, however, help control the problem.

Dr. Benjamin F. Feingold, a pediatric allergist, theorized that certain food additives can cause or worsen hyperactivity. The list of suspect additives includes artificial food colors and flavors, salicylates (aspirin-like compounds), and antioxidants such as BHA and BHT. The Feingold Diet carefully screens out these food ingredients. Many parents have tried the diet and report success in controlling their children's behavior.

Controlled studies[1], however, suggest that the

typical hyperactive child does not have a food sensitivity or allergy to these food ingredients. The child grows no worse when given the additive experimentally, and acts no better when it is removed. What, then, about the parental reports of success?

First, there may be psychological principles at work rather than nutritional ones. Parents who focus more attention on their unruly kids may see behavioral improvement regardless of what they feed them.

Second, some studies suggest that a small proportion of hyperactive children may truly be sensitive or allergic to certain food additives. For them, relief may be found in the elimination of those additives.

Finally, we know that caffeine activates the system, and many children consume far too much caffeine from soda and chocolate, as well as coffee or tea. As Table 3.3 indicates, even the teen who avoids coffee and tea can get just as much caffeine as his parents from other sources.

Reducing caffeine intake in children seems a sound idea. Parents need only to substitute caffeine-free sodas for caffeinated ones, avoid serving coffee to children, and reduce excessive chocolate intake. Because the Feingold Diet forbids many healthy foods such as fruits and vegetables, this book does not recommend the entire plan. Nor does it suggest that even the best parts of the diet

TABLE 3.3
CAFFEINE AMOUNTS (IN MILLIGRAMS)
IN STANDARD SERVINGS OF:

Ground coffee	80–150
Instant coffee	40–110
Brewed tea	20–100
Iced tea	20–35
Cola soda (1 can)	30–50
Chocolate (2 ounces)	20–40
Hot chocolate	5

will help all hyperactive children. However, some children may be allergic to some food additives. Identifying and removing from the diet the specific troublesome compounds does make good sense. But do not attempt this process alone. Consult a physician who can carefully test one suspect food at a time to see if it causes a problem.

Natural Food Toxins

Artificial additives and contaminants are not the only—nor even the major—health threat in food. Thousands of chemical compounds occur naturally in food, some of which are more potent and dangerous than those artificial additives banned by the FDA. Yet most of these are unavoidable unless you refuse to eat all the foods that contain them. In fact, no food is free of all possible natural hazards. This statement is not meant to alarm but only to put the discussion of artificial additives into proper perspective.

Even some compounds that are criticized as additives also occur naturally in foods. For instance, nitrates are found naturally in such vegetables as lettuce, radishes, and spinach. Nitrites occur naturally in human saliva. As additives, both compounds are used to improve color in cured meat and inhibit growth of deadly botulin bacteria. Too much of nitrates and nitrites is toxic, however. And stomach acids can convert even small amounts of nitrite into nitrosamines, which may increase cancer risk. Table 3.4 lists some types of natural-food hazards.

• *Herbal Alkaloids.* Some teens avoid tea and coffee to skip the caffeine but then drink various

---

TABLE 3.4
SOME TYPES OF NATURAL
FOOD HAZARDS

Herbal Alkaloids
Mycotoxins
Natural Carcinogens
Natural Pesticides

---

herbal teas without a second thought. Unfortunately, some herbs naturally contain compounds with much more serious effects than caffeine. Just as your body contains many enzymes, hormones, and other compounds, plants develop their own chemicals. Over the centuries primitive peoples have discovered the medicinal value of many plants. For instance, the Chippewa Indians used prairie clover for heart problems and wild ginger for indigestion. Modern science has determined that chemicals within those plants are responsible for some of these medicinal effects. Some chemicals in herbs with the most potent effects on consumers are *alkaloids*. These substances are alkaline (able to neutralize acids) and contain nitrogen. Many are purified and used as drugs—either legal such as atropine and quinine, or illegal, such as cocaine.

The alkaloids in herbs can dissolve in the water when one brews herbal teas. The consumer of such teas has no idea which "drugs" or how much of them is being drunk. And some teens are sensitive or even allergic to these chemicals. Yet because they are natural compounds, the FDA does not analyze or regulate them. Consumers must decide for themselves.

People allergic to ragweed, for instance, often are allergic to chamomile tea, which is similar chemically. Comfrey tea can damage the liver; jimson or nutmeg tea can harm the nervous system and vision; kavakava tea affects the skin and hearing. Some teas derive from the same herbs as prescription medicines. These include foxglove, which provides digitalis, a substance prescribed for heart patients but capable of causing heart attacks in those with normal hearts. Melilot, tonka bean, and woodruff teas all contain coumarin, used as a blood thinner to dissolve blood clots, but which causes excessive bleeding in normal people. Snakeroot contains reserpine, which affects the nervous system. As an example of how dangerous some natural chemicals can be, consider that President Abraham Lincoln's mother died after drinking milk from a cow which had eaten snakeroot!

• *Mycotoxins.* "Myco" refers to fungus and "toxin" to poison. Accordingly, these poisons are created in foods by molds and other fungi. The mold does not have to be visible to produce toxins. The worst of these poisons is aflatoxin, already discussed. Other mycotoxins include ergot and patulin. These mycotoxins occur most frequently in peanuts, corn, and other grains that have been stored too long in a moist environment. They can also end up in dairy products if cows have eaten the infested grain. To minimize your own mycotoxin exposure at home:

> Store foods in sealed containers and/or the refrigerator.

> Don't eat peanut shells; toss out old nuts.

Dump yogurt, cream cheese, or other soft cheese with visible mold. (For hard cheeses, you can trim out one-half inch all around the mold and eat the rest.)

Dispose of bread containing mold.

• *Natural Carcinogens.* A carcinogen is any item that increases your chances of developing cancer. Natural carcinogens include hydrazines in edible mushrooms, psoralens in celery and parsley, safrole in black pepper, and solanine in potatoes. The last-mentioned is the only one you can reduce without having to avoid the food altogether. Solanine appears in the green patches on potatoes, so cut off and discard those from whole potatoes and potato chips. (Don't be alarmed if you eat a little solanine. It would take several pounds of potato green to actually kill you.)

The fact that some plant foods contain carcinogens does NOT mean we should avoid eating them. These same plants also contain many essential nutrients and anticarcinogens, chemicals that help your body resist cancer. Carrots alone contain over thirty chemicals that help fight cancer. Broccoli contains sulforaphane, which helps living cells destroy or expel carcinogens. All plants that contain the vitamins A, C, and E help resist cancer. Public-health studies demonstrate conclusively that the net effect of consuming fruits, vegetables, and grain products is highly beneficial.

• *Natural Pesticides.* Some teens think of pesticides as noxious sprays manufactured by chemical companies and laced heavily on our produce by greedy farmers who want to squeeze every last penny from their fields. But did you know that plants naturally create their own chemical pesticides to ward off insects and other animal predators and to resist the growth of mold? These compounds do not put off all pests, but they still exist in the plants and become part of our food supply. In fact, the toxicologist Dr. Bruce Ames[2] estimates that we consume about 10,000 times more of such natural pesticides than we do of artificial pesticide residues. We can forget the notion that artificial spells danger while natural ensures safety. But remember that the net effect of eating plant foods is positive because they contain so many anticarcinogens and essential nutrients.

What You Can Do

Now that you know about the risks of food additives—both natural and synthesized—you might fear that your next trip to the supermarket will be more like entering a maze filled with potential hazards and wrong choices. It needn't be. Here are some general guidelines regarding food additives that you can follow.

• The best way to avoid overexposure to unwanted food additives is to avoid processed convenience foods. Sure, it takes more time to toss a fresh salad than to nuke a frozen pizza in the microwave. But the salad is healthier and will leave you feeling more energized. A fresh whole apple is better for you than a packaged apple pie. A slice of whole wheat or homemade bread beats a cookie.

• Avoid excess of any one food or food component, such as sweets, salt, or caffeine. Seek a balanced diet instead.

• If you discover you are sensitive or allergic to any food or additive, be careful to avoid that in the future.

4

Are Pesticides Poisoning Our Food Supply?

Natural-food toxins don't make good press because we can't do much about them. But when some human-made chemical is linked to disease, banner headlines splash across the front pages of newspapers nationwide.

For instance, in 1989, a non-profit environmental group called the National Resources Defense Council reported that alar, a compound sprayed on apples to combat fungus, had been linked with cancer. Long-term ingestion of alar, estimates indicate, could cause one cancer case for every 4,200 preschool children. (Older children and adults can better handle this substance and are little affected by it.) This is much greater than the usually accepted risk of one case per million people.

Several federal bureaus disagreed with the report, but the public reacted with alarm bordering on panic. Throughout the nation, people refused to eat apples for a time, leaving them to rot on supermarket shelves. From the initial public reaction, one would have thought that alar is the scariest, most potent threat to health and safety in the entire food supply. In reality, it is just one small threat among thousands of other small threats.

But alar was the one threat singled out by the media at the time. The news commotion conveniently ignored the fact that only 5 percent of apple growers even used alar in the first place. The media also overlooked the fact that shunning all apples or other fruits presents more dietary dangers in the long run than chomping down an occasional bit of alar. In response, the apple industry agreed to minimize the use of alar, and the public's attention soon turned to the next "health hazard of the week" publicity campaign. The next time you encounter a "food scare" such as this, try to focus more on facts than on emotions.

From such media cries of alarm one might get the notion that farmers are deliberately trying to poison us. But pesticide use is intended for beneficial reasons. Even with thousands of natural pesticides and widespread use of human-made pesticides, about one-third of the world's crops are lost to insects and other pests. This not only represents a severe economic loss, but reduces our ability to feed the world's poor and hungry. Therefore, farmers use chemical toxins to kill or ward off insects (insecticides), prevent fungus infestation (fungicides), and reduce the growth of competing plants such as weeds (herbicides). In fact, farmers apply nearly two billion pounds of pesticides per year to their crops.

Can this massive chemical bath harm us?

Pesticide Risks

If a pesticide sprayed on a food disappears before that food reaches the market, there would be no direct threat to human health. Some pesticides do break down chemically after prolonged exposure to sunlight, air, and water. However, some of the resulting metabolites—chemical by-products— may also be toxic to humans. Also, some pesticides remain unchanged in the soil, where they can be absorbed into the plant or possibly contaminate groundwater sources.

The normal, healthy teen or adult can eat a certain amount of pesticides and pesticide metabolites with little concern. The liver can chemically break down a wide variety of toxins, including many pesticides and such chemicals as alcohol, which is how an intoxicated person sobers up. But just as drinking faster than the liver can react leads to drunkenness, ingesting more pesticide than the system can handle causes illness. Furthermore, some toxins harm the liver, and others can't be

---

TABLE 4.1
CONCENTRATION OF TOXINS IN ORGANISMS,
FROM LOWER TO HIGHER

A teenager—100 pounds
(1 gram of toxin per 100 pounds)

A beef cow—1,000 pounds
(1/10 gram of toxin per 100 pounds)

Hay, grass, or feed grains—several tons
($^1/_{100}$ gram of toxin per 100 pounds)

Note: Higher organisms over time eat more
than their own weight of lower organisms, thus
accumulating persistent toxins. This does
not apply to toxins that break down rapidly.

---

broken down by this organ. Persistent pesticides such as DDT concern us the most, for their total amounts in the body keep building every time we are exposed to them.

The problem gets worse in higher organisms, such as humans. Humans eat both plants and lower organisms. These lower organisms, such as cows, themselves contain pesticide residues (see Table 4.1). Overexposure to pesticides can, in sensitive people, cause such problems as:

- Sterility
- Genetic damage and birth defects

- Cancer
- Damage to the nervous system and other organs
- Death

The experience of the former Soviet Union illustrates the terrible hazards of long-term, uncontrolled pesticide use. Studies done during the early 1990s showed that in Latvia, for instance, pesticides killed 14,000 and caused diseases in about 700,000 people per year. Studies also suggested that whole regions in Russia have become so toxic from pesticides and industrial wastes that nearly everyone living there suffers ill health as a result.

In modern democracies, however, serious pesticide poisoning occurs mostly in medical research on deliberate overexposure in animals or in overexposure in humans, such as chemical factory workers or farmers, who experience accidents with pesticides. The average American consumer eating normal foods over a lifetime has only a minimal exposure to pesticides, and this presents little direct hazard. Even a moderate direct dose may cause only short-term effects. For instance, a home gardener getting one whiff too many of a pesticide may experience only some temporary irritation of the eyes, nose, or mouth. If the exposure is heavy enough and continues over time, however, the pesticide does build up.

In addition to whatever exposure we suffer as individuals, we should all be concerned about possible threats to our environment. DDT was commonly used as a pesticide for many years until the widespread severity of its damage became known. Rachel Carson's book *Silent Spring* , in 1962, helped to make the public aware of the dangers of uncontrolled pesticide use. Pesticides can kill not only the intended targets but many beneficial insects (such as bees) and other wildlife.

The more we use pesticides, the more pests develop resistance to them. This means that various species become hardy enough to survive a given pesticide. It then becomes useless against that species, and other pesticides must be developed to achieve the intended results. Thus the quest for different and more lethal pesticides continues.

In this war between pests and people, who defends the consumer?

Pesticide Regulations

Both the EPA (Environmental Protection Agency) and the FDA (Food and Drug Administration) share the responsibility of regulating pesticide use to protect the nation's food supply.

EPA Responsibilities. The EPA registers all allowable pesticides according to provisions of the Federal Insecticide, Fungicide, and Rodenticide Act (FIFRA). It is illegal to use on crops a pesticide that is not on the EPA list. Before a manufacturer can sell a newly developed pesticide, it must apply for EPA registration. The EPA also sets the maximum levels of pesticide residues allowed on crops at the time of their harvesting. Ideally, no residues would be left when a crop hits the market, but pesticides have a way of persisting beyond their period of use.

Recognizing the problem of persistence, the EPA conducts risk assessment studies to determine what levels are reasonably safe. The EPA's first step for each pesticide is to determine the No Observable Effect Level (NOEL). This is the maximum amount of pesticide residues that causes no health problems in animal studies. As a safety measure, NOEL is divided by 100 to set the Acceptable Daily Intake (ADI) level for humans. This safety margin takes into account that humans may be more sensitive than animals to a given pesticide. And some humans are more sensitive than others. The EPA also estimates how much of a given pesticide people actually consume based on residue tests of produce. If this estimate falls above the safe level (ADI), then the EPA must take action to reduce residue levels.

Control becomes somewhat more complicated than this with pesticides capable of causing cancer.

Because of the Delaney Clause, no additive linked with cancer is considered acceptable in human foods. Since pesticides are considered a type of food additive, the Delaney Clause should hold, at least in theory. In reality, however, the regulations have so many loopholes that pesticides registered before 1978 are allowed even though they pose some minimal cancer risk. Ironic, isn't it? The Delaney provision prevents new pesticides from being introduced, but does not rid us of some older pesticides, even if they're more dangerous. Further scientific and legal work remains to be done in this area.

• *FDA Responsibilities.* The FDA monitors the levels of pesticide residues in fresh produce brought to market to ensure that safety levels are not exceeded. Unfortunately, limitations on the size of the FDA mean that it can screen no more than one percent of the foreign and domestic produce reaching American markets. However, as a second safety measure, the FDA checks residues in cooked food. It periodically buys food from a handful of regular grocery stores and prepares it for consumption just as a consumer would, and then checks it again. For the most part such studies indicate that by the time the produce reaches the brown bags in your station wagon or your dining room table, the pesticide levels have declined well below the Acceptable Daily Intakes established by the EPA. In other words, all of us are probably eating some human-made pesticide residues, but the amounts are so low as to pose very little risk.

Lingering Concerns
Over Pesticide Use

Nevertheless, pesticides do pose threats. What are some concerns over pesticide use?

• Pesticide risks are greatest for young children, babies, and the unborn due to the pregnant woman's diet. The younger the individuals, the less developed are their organs. This makes them susceptible to damage and means that they have less ability to detoxify ingested pesticides. Young children's or infants' low body weight also means that a given dose is more concentrated.

• What about risks of pesticide exposure other than through food? Most studies focus only on food rather than contaminated air or water.

• What about interactions among different pesticides? How do pesticides react with other environmental contaminants? If pesticide residue x causes two units of harm, and pesticide y causes three units, does exposure to both result in five units? This is not a matter of simple addition, because some chemicals have *synergy*—that is, their effects when combined are stronger than the sum of their separate effects. This means that you might get six or eight units of harm from a combination of x and y instead of five. In fact, the combination of malathion, used to kill fruit flies, and some other organic phosphate pesticides is fifty times as potent as their simple sum!

• Are "organically" grown foods really safer as often claimed? The term "organic" usually refers to foods grown by natural methods—without artificial fertilizers and pesticides. There is no meaning specified by law, however, so organic can mean anything a dealer wants it to. Unscrupulous food producers or merchants sometimes trick the public into paying more for supposedly "organic" lettuce or oranges that are really the same as those found at the nearest grocery. Even farmers honestly trying to grow organic crops may raise them close enough to sprayed fields that some pesticides drift over to them also. If crops come from a field certified as pesticide-free, however, they should contain less pesticide residues than typical produce. If pesticides concern you, and you can afford such certified foods, it won't hurt to try them.

Alternatives to
Chemical Pesticides

But what if you can't avoid foods with pesticides? What other options is science working on?

In the future we may develop biodegradable pesticides, those that break down to harmless chemicals by the time of harvesting. Meanwhile, because persistent chemical insecticides do present a risk to human health, scientists keep trying to develop alternative ways to control crop pests. These methods of biological warfare include:

• *Sterilization*. It might sound odd, but this approach to reducing insect populations involves breeding more insects on purpose, then sterilizing them. When these sterile insects are released, many mate with normal insects, preventing them from reproducing as well. Despite a temporary increase in the number of insects, therefore, there should be a sharp decline in the next generation.

• *Pheromones*. These are natural chemicals used by one sex to attract the other of the same species. Farmers can use pheromones produced artificially to lure insect pests not to mates but to traps or pesticides.

• *Rival Species*. Many insect species are the favorite targets of predators. By introducing or increasing the population of predators in a region, the numbers of the target pest can be kept down. Of course, agricultural experts must be careful not to choose a predator species that will present other problems to crops or people.

• *Pest Diseases*. Pest species are also susceptible to various bacterial and viral diseases. Provided they are not dangerous to humans or other animals, such microbes can be bred and introduced in an area to subdue the pest population there.

• *Pest-Resistant Plants*. Plants can produce their

own natural pesticides. Cross-breeding can sometimes produce plant varieties that are even more resistant to insects. For example, scientists have developed a new "hairy potato" hybrid with aboveground leaves that are thick and shaggy and keep out or trap all the normal insects that attack potatoes. The consumer, of course, does not eat the covering—it is left behind during harvesting. Another way to improve plant varieties is by genetic engineering. Scientists are working on ways to insert desirable insect-resisting genes into various edible plant species.

• *Crop Rotation.* Planting different crops in the same field on alternate years can reduce pest damage. If tomato worms infest a given field, for example, they tend to remain year after year. But if the farmer plants a different crop that tomato worms can't eat, the infestation will die out naturally the following year.

• *Genetically Engineered Biopesticides.* This is the newest weapon in the pesticide arsenal. Scientists have genetically engineered new bacterial strains that are deadly to insects but not to other forms of animal life including humans. According to some, the danger of these biopesticides is that they might mutate on their own into new forms that are dangerous to valuable animals or humans. Biopesticides can reduce the amount of chemical pesticides dumped into the environment, but they may present previously unknown hazards if allowed to reproduce freely in the wild. To minimize this danger, scientists breed new bacteria, kill them, then spread them over crops. The toxins in the dead bacteria still kill the insects, which swallow them but don't threaten the environment.

Using a variety of alternative methods like these is known as Integrated Pest Management. A study by the National Research Council[3] proved that such methods can keep crop yields high without the use of chemical pesticides.

Minimizing Pesticide Risks at Home

Not all pesticides are applied commercially. Home gardeners in the United States also apply about 80 million pounds of pesticides annually. Could these present a health hazard, too? A study by the National Cancer Institute found the rates of childhood leukemia to be more than six times higher in the offspring of mothers who used pesticides at home during pregnancy or nursing as compared with offspring of mothers who did not. Rates of some other diseases may also increase.

If you or your family love to plant rows of juicy tomatoes, crispy lettuce, and bright squash, think about minimizing your exposure to pesticides:
- First, choose a garden plot without prior pes-

ticide exposure. If you can't avoid one already soaked in the stuff, the first year consider planting alfalfa, clover, or some other non-food plant that will absorb the pesticide residues in the ground. Discard that harvest and start your food crops the next year.

• Also choose a plot that does not lie immediately downwind or downhill from a neighbor who uses pesticides. You don't want your neighbor's pesticides to blow or wash off into your plot.

• Don't use pesticides unless necessary. If a disease or insect pest appears, don't start throwing chemicals at it. Select a treatment specific to that problem.

• Use only pesticides approved for use on fruits and vegetables.

• Read the pesticide labels completely before applying anything. Follow the directions carefully and use no more than you have to. Calibrate your sprayer so you dispense only the correct amount.

• Store pesticides in their original containers to avoid accidental contamination. Keep these out of the reach of children and pets. Dispose of empty pesticide containers carefully.

• Apply pesticides only when there is little wind.

• While administering the pesticide, wear a hat, long-sleeve shirt, gloves, and boots (preferably rubber ones) or outdoor shoes that you won't use inside.

• Wear a face mask while using an airborne spray. Buy the kind that hooks a surgical cup over your nose and mouth with elastic. Or at least tie a bandanna over your nose and mouth.

• Invest also in safety goggles if you plan to do much spraying.

• Don't apply pesticides when you're the only one home. If you get poisoned, you may grow dizzy, vomit, have trouble walking, or feel confused. You may need help to get to a hospital.

• Wash up carefully after handling pesticides— but not in the kitchen! If you've used an airborne spray, dump your clothes (in the wash) right afterward and head for the shower. Wash your hair, too.

• Dispose of pesticide containers properly.

• Before consuming the fruits and vegetables you grew, wash them thoroughly (see end of next section).

What Else You Can Do

If you don't grow your own fruits and vegetables, you can still minimize your exposure to pesticide residues if that problem concerns you.

• Buy so-called "organic" food from reputable dealers you can trust to offer produce only from untreated fields.

• When you can't do the above, buy produce from local farmers or farmers' markets where the growers are up-front about their pest management methods and you can trust them.

• Buy produce from large supermarket chains that have good reputations for safe food.

• If there is any chance your produce was exposed to pesticides, scrub and rinse it carefully before use. Throw away the outer leaves of lettuce, cabbage, and similar items. Throw away the peel on apples, squash, potatoes, and such items if you suspect a problem or if they look waxy, since wax can seal in pesticides.

Ultimately, the risks posed by pesticides used at home resemble those posed by pesticides applied commercially. There's no way to completely avoid hazard, but with knowledge and a little planning you can minimize it.

5

Controversial Agricultural and Food-Processing Techniques

Like a Little Hormones in Your Steak?

You've heard of athletes illegally building muscle by taking hormones—chemical messengers that control many bodily functions, including muscle growth. But did you know that farmers lace cattle feed with hormones to add bulk to their livestock's muscles too? Animal muscle provides salable meat, so the more of it that farmers can produce, the more they can sell. Growth hormones also increase milk yields. Hormones cost little but increase profits significantly.

This method of agriculture has its dangers, however, as the case of diethylstilbestrol (DES) reveals. During the 1960s many farmers used DES, a synthetic hormone in the feed of steers. Cattle gained about 10 percent more weight, producing more lean meat on less feed. But the farmers' dream turned into a nightmare when studies revealed that daughters of women taking DES as a medicine to stabilize pregnancy had an increased rate of vaginal cancer. Even though consuming DES in meat was not directly linked to this problem, the Delaney Clause was invoked and DES was banned in animal feed during the 1970s.

Other hormones are used today to stimulate animal growth. Do these hormones leave residues in meat for human diners to consume later? Can these molecular messengers alter biochemical processes in the human consumer too? There hasn't been enough research in this area to answer these questions definitively. Most such hormones, however, should break down chemically between the time of last dosing and ultimate consumption of the meat. In addition, the strongest concentration occurs where the hormone—given to the animal as an implant—was set. Normally this is behind the ear because it does not produce edible meat.

Studies do indicate some hormone residues in some meat, but this is usually at levels far below those produced normally in the human body. Furthermore, most hormones when eaten break down chemically during digestion. However, isolated instances of the use of uncontrolled or illegal hormones in animal feed have caused medical problems in some human consumers. Such hormone use does pose a risk, but it is generally well controlled.

How About Antibiotics When You Aren't Sick?

If you get a strep throat or other bacterial infection, your doctor will normally prescribe antibiotics—drugs that can destroy or weaken invading bacteria. Farmers discovered that animals fed antibiotics along with their oats or hay grew faster and larger than others. For a small investment in pills, the farmer could reap greater profits through increased meat production. Antibiotics mixed with feed for hens also improve the size and quality of eggs.

Like taking antibiotics when you're not sick, this practice carries several risks, however.

• *Development of resistant bacteria.* Many experts believe that unnecessary use of antibiotics leads to antibiotic-resistant bacteria. Widespread overuse provides more opportunities for strains of bacteria to mutate into forms less sensitive to the antibiotic. The more a certain antibiotic is used, the less effective it will become in the long run. Antibiotics that formerly were highly effective against certain strains of human disease now have little effect. In addition, applying a useless antibiotic may actually encourage the growth of a resistant bacterial strain by wiping out its more sensitive competitors. Medical scientists, in turn, must respond by developing newer, stronger antibiotics. Eventually, bacterial strains may develop that are resistant to these, too. Continually the battle rages between scientific improvements in antibiotics and the evolution of new strains of bacteria. Some believe that any unnecessary use of antibiotics merely gives the bacterial world an advantage in this war. Are increased farmer profits and lower consumer prices worth it?

• *Possible effects on human health.* We know that antibiotics in animal feed can make their way into meat as an unintended food additive and that, over time, they break down chemically. Antibiotics can also be destroyed by heat in cooking. However, a certain amount of residues could be consumed from animal products. This could trigger allergic reactions, even serious ones, in people sensitive to these drugs, which may include about one-tenth of the American population. Other people may experience unpleasant side effects from antibiotic consumption, such as nausea, cramps, and diarrhea. In addition, an excess of antibiotics can kill off many of the normal bacteria in the intestine that produce vitamin K, which could lead to a deficiency of this vitamin.

To protect against these health concerns, the FDA has established drug administration cut-off dates before animal slaughtering. This withdrawal period allows the amount of antibiotics in the animal flesh to decline to a negligible level before salable meat reaches the market.

Nuke Your Food and Eat It, Too

Like the use of antibiotics in growing food, the use of radiation in preparing it affects the consumer. Most of us already consume some foods that have been nuked, whether we know it or not. Yet many of us would gasp to think of it.

Ever since the first A-bomb mushroom clouds darkened the skies, we have lived with the fear of nuclear radiation. In fiction and nonfiction stories alike we learn of radiation exposure triggering horrible side effects such as hair loss, cancer, destruction of nervous tissue, and death.

But the same gamma rays that can sterilize, deform, or kill a human can thoroughly zap the bacteria, viruses, and destructive enzymes in a package of food. Preparing food through radiation sounds like space-age magic: Cook a meal. Seal it in plastic. Zap it with radiation. With all the germs dead, it stays fresh, tasty, and safe—practically forever, or until you open the package.

Do consumers have reason to fear the use of radiation on food? Could it cause cancer or terrible genetic mutations, they wonder? There are two sides to the issue.

The PRO side:

• Nuking food with radiation does not make it radioactive. Rads, or units of radiation, kill the microbes (germs) that spoil food but do not make the food give off further radiation.

• Radiation also kills food parasites and bacteria that can make consumers sick, thus improving health. The FDA now allows the use of radiation to kill trichinosis (porkworm) parasites, to kill micro-organisms on herbs and spices, and to control insects in grain.

• Radiation of food could make it possible to use fewer chemical treatments on food, reducing the need for pesticides, preservatives, and the like.

• Since it increases shelf life, radiation can lessen food spoilage and lower costs.

The CON Side:

• Radiating food does cause biochemical changes called *radiolytic products*. Most of these have been known to science for years because heat and other processing produces them, too. However, about 10 percent of radiolytic products are caused uniquely by radiation and are not found in foods prepared in other ways. Tests suggest that these are not dangerous, but we can't rule out all risk. Who knows what long-term, heavy consumption might reveal in future decades?

• Handling nuclear materials for food irradiation creates safety problems in storage, use, and disposal of nuclear waste.

• Some nutrients are lost during irradiation, though this happens with all other processing methods, too.

• People are scared of anything nuclear, and most consumers won't knowingly buy irradiated foods. As long as public opinion remains so negative, it is unlikely that commercial uses of irradiation will become much more common than they are today.

Cooking
Kills Nutrients

What, then, is the best way to raise and prepare food? To get the maximum nutritional benefit from fruits and vegetables, you would need your own garden. Then you could pluck oranges and tomatoes just before eating them since any delay in use after harvesting leads to a gradual breakdown of vitamins.

But once you began to cook your specially grown food, you'd diminish its nutritional value.

TABLE 5.1
VITAMIN C LOSSES IN GREEN PEAS
DUE TO PROCESSING

Method	Vitamin C Lost
Eat fresh	0%
Canned, eat cold	37%
Cooked fresh	56%
Frozen, then cooked	61%
Canned, then cooked	64%

Any kind of processing, particularly with high heat, destroys some nutrients. Don't be overly concerned, however. Even canned and frozen foods still contain much of their original nutrient worth. The big food companies are aware of the problems and try to minimize them. For instance, they'll often harvest green peas and process them right in the field, freezing them as soon as possible to reduce nutrient loss. For examples of nutrient loss from cooking, see Table 5.1.

Are Natural Fertilizers
Better Than Artificial Ones?

Say you were going to grow your own garden. Would your fertilizer affect your food? Some teens believe that artificial fertilizers can't possibly be as good as natural ones. But the oat and wheat plants that draw nutrients from them can't tell whether these nitrogen-containing compounds were collected naturally or manufactured artificially. A chemical molecule is the same regardless of source. The plant will use either in the same way. However, both types of fertilizers do contain some risk. Natural fertilizers such as manure or animal feces may carry disease-producing bacteria or other contaminants. And artificial ones may carry production contaminants. Farmers, therefore, generally go for the source that is relatively cheap and readily available, and you would probably do the same.

Are Organic Foods Superior to Regular Ones?

What if you were an organic farmer? Would you take greater pride in your food's purity? Organic foods may contain less pesticide residues if they come from a reputable source. However, organic foods are not more nutritious and may cost more. Your body can't distinguish between calcium or vitamin C from organic broccoli versus regular broccoli. Superiority is often in the eye of the beholder. If consumers think that organic is better, then they will feel better buying and eating that.

Murphy's Law in Action:
Accidental Contamination

Not all food risks come from additives or pesticides applied deliberately. Sometimes accidents contaminate the food supply. As Murphy's Law states, if anything can go wrong, it will. For instance, in 1968 in Japan an accidental contamination of rice-bran cooking oil poisoned over 1,000 people with PCB's (polychlorinated biphenyls), which chemically resemble the deadly pesticide DDT. Ironically, the contamination occurred in the factory during a heating process intended to purify the oil. The pipes used in heating contained PCB's and were old, with tiny holes that leaked the PCB's into the oil. No one discovered the contamination until people using the oil in cooking experienced serious health effects such as joint swelling and pain, acne, eyelid secretions, liver disease, and genetic defects. To avoid these kinds of accidents, food manufacturing plants must be checked regularly by impartial government inspectors with the power to order changes. There is little the individual consumer can do in such cases. Many contaminants cannot be detected directly by the human senses. Once a batch of a product is discovered by government authorities to have a problem, they'll issue public warnings and recalls of that batch. So keeping up with the news is a good idea.

6

Is Your Kitchen Making You Sick?

Consumers must face the fact that no matter how careful farmers, animal slaughterhouses, food warehouses, shippers, and handlers are, food will be exposed to some bacteria and contaminants. Some of the food you buy will carry unpleasant guests you can't see, smell, or taste directly.

What you do after the food enters your home, however, plays a large role in whether or not this contamination will make you sick. Careful handling on your part can overcome many of the hazards that creep in during food production. Conversely, a sloppy disregard for safety can greatly increase your chances of acquiring a foodborne infection or other health hazard. These range in severity from minor, temporary flulike symptoms to severe life-threatening diseases.

Types of Disease Carried by Food

• *Foodborne Infections.* When the live bacteria or viruses from food directly invade your system after consumption, multiply, and make you sick, you contract what we call a foodborne infection. Eating contaminated foods raw greatly increases your risk of getting one. For example, raw clams and oysters from polluted waters spread hepatitis, a severe liver disease. Proper cooking can eliminate this threat entirely by killing the offending microbes. Other examples include salmonella and shigellosis infections, which can be spread from a sick person to a well one through food.

• *Foodborne Intoxications.* When bacteria produce toxins in food that can sicken the consumer, we call that a foodborne intoxication. After the toxins have been produced, even killing the bacteria won't eliminate this threat. Cooking may kill the microbes, but not disable the toxins. Luckily, cooking does destroy botulism toxin, the most deadly type of food poisoning known.

• *Parasites.* Parasitic worms can infect the human body in many ways. The key dietary entry points are through infected foods or beverages. For example, porkworms (trichina) can enter hogs that feed in contaminated areas. The worms produce tiny cysts in the muscles of the hogs. When the infected animals are butchered and the meat is brought to market, it still contains the worm cysts. These cysts will survive partial or inadequate cooking. If a human then eats that pork, the cysts will mature and release their worms into the human's gut. The tiny larvae will travel throughout the body and burrow into the human's muscles, causing pain, fever, and other symptoms. In a similar way, human consumers can ingest beef tapeworms or fish worms.

To combat the parasite problem, farmers need to raise their animals in areas as free as possible from parasites. But you as a consumer can never be 100 percent certain that the meat or fish you buy is parasite-free. Most worm eggs and cysts are too small to detect without a microscope. The only way to be safe is to thoroughly cook fish and meat (especially pork) before eating it. The idea of eating worm eggs and cysts even if they're dead seems disgusting, but at least they won't infect you. Many people like to eat very rare steaks, raw meat, or raw fish (*sushi*), but a number of them have contracted parasites as a result.

What You Can Do

Here are tips to help you prevent your kitchen—and others' kitchens—from making you sick.

• *Buy from reputable dealers.* If raw animal foods turn you on, you can cut your chances of infection by dealing only with the most reputable markets and restaurants. One survey of fresh cod, for example, found 90 percent of the fish infected. But trained, responsible *sushi* dealers take steps to protect their customers. For example, saltwater fish are less likely than freshwater ones to have parasites, so *sushi* usually is made from ocean varieties. Getting the freshest fish helps, as does gutting them promptly since most parasites live in the gut. A good *sushi* chef can spot parasites during food preparation and will throw out that fish or marinate it in salt and vinegar to kill the wrigglers. If you suspect you've been infected, however, don't panic. See your doctor, who can test you for parasites and treat you if you have them.

• *Avoid contaminating food.* Handling food when you have a cold, flu, or infected skin can plant your germs in food. Under certain temperature conditions the bacteria will multiply rapidly and cause food poisoning when eaten. When you have open sores or communicable diseases, don't handle food intended for others. If you are sick, don't even handle your own food until you are ready to eat it. Even though you already have the type of germs you'll pass to your food through contact, in food they can multiply fast enough to create additional problems for you.

• *Avoid spreading contamination.* Raw chicken and other meats frequently contain bacteria. Wash thoroughly anything that touches that meat—your hands, a knife, a cutting board—before letting it touch any other food. Don't use the same utensils to handle the food when raw and later when cooked unless you wash them in between.

• *Keep your kitchen clean.* Don't wait until food junk resembles a Chia Pet before tossing it out of the refrigerator and pantry. Don't let dirty dishes pile up in the food-handling areas of the kitchen.

• *Follow the 40–140 rule.* Cold foods should be kept below 40 degrees Fahrenheit, so refrigerate leftovers promptly. Cold keeps most bacteria from multiplying but won't usually kill them. Keep hot foods above 140 degrees, which also prevents most bacteria from multiplying. Don't leave out hot leftovers to gradually cool down on the counter, but refrigerate them quickly, preferably in a container with a large surface area to promote faster cooling. Foods left out in the open between 40 and 140 degrees provide fertile breeding grounds for bacteria and viruses. Exposed to the air, foods also collect dust and grow stale quickly due to oxygen and light. Keep foods at these temperatures for no longer than two hours. Be especially careful with protein foods such as ham salad, chicken salad, and egg salad in which bacteria seem to thrive.

• *Thaw food carefully.* Thaw frozen foods in the refrigerator (that is, under 40 degrees) or microwave them rather than allowing them to sit at room temperature, which favors the growth of bacteria already in the food.

• *Kill germs and parasites.* Freezing food, even at low temperatures, does not kill many bacteria, though it will chill them into an inactive state. Only high temperatures can actually kill these disease-causing microorganisms and parasites. For example, don't eat pork that is still rare enough to be pink or reddish. Cook it until it turns at least grayish. Terminate any possible germs and worms!

• *Throw out bad food.* If food looks or smells bad, don't take a chance—throw it out. Better to waste it that way than to throw it up later from illness. Don't even taste suspicious foods. With strong food poisons, one taste can harm you. A single taste of food poisoned with botulism can kill!

7

Leveling with the American Consumer: *Food Labels*

Until this century, even the experts knew little about the chemicals composing foods and how they support human health and functioning. The average consumer buying food in the first half of this century knew next to nothing about nutritional values. People were guided in their food purchases mostly by availability, personal preference, cost, and such homespun wisdom as "an apple a day keeps the doctor away" and "eat your vegetables, they're good for you."

Finally, in the 1970s, advances in nutritional knowledge and mounting consumer interest led to a demand for more informative food labeling. The FDA developed regulations that specified the form and minimum content of labels. All food labels had to state the name of the item and its ingredients in descending order by weight, the most prevalent one being listed first. If the manufacturer enriched the product by adding nutrients or made any nutritional claims about it, the label then had to include complete nutritional information. Otherwise a listing of nutritional contents was optional. Food manufacturers generally flaunted on labels a nutrient profile that they thought looked good but left off one that didn't smack of health. Most dessert and snack foods, for instance, generally lacked nutritional statements.

If used, nutritional statements on food labels by law included the serving size, the calories in each portion, the grams of protein, fat, and carbohydrate in each serving, and the major nutrients as a percentage of the U.S. Recommended Dietary Allowances (U.S. RDA). (See Table 7.1 later in this chapter for a sample label.) These U.S. RDA numbers indicate the best estimates among nutritionists of the daily intake of each key nutrient needed to support health and effectiveness in the vast majority of people. A large margin of safety was built in by selecting the highest value of each nutrient from all the recommended values for different age categories.

Problems in
the System

The labeling system that survived until the early 1990s left so many loopholes that even NUTRO-MIGHT could get confused.

- *Bogus serving sizes.* Many companies kept their serving sizes unnaturally small so that they could report fewer calories and grams of fat in each. Does the average person really get two servings out of one can of soda, two and a half from a small can of soup, and three from a candy bar? Accuracy required the consumer to adjust the reported figures by their actual serving size, clearly a difficult task.
- *Deceptive health claims.* Whatever nutrition fad or concern was sweeping the nation at any given time usually was reflected in labels. When cholesterol was a big item in the news, many labels proclaimed "CHOLESTEROL FREE!" Many customers assumed that the food had been improved and made safer by the reduction of cholesterol. Usually, however, the label was applied to plant foods that never had any cholesterol to begin with. (Cholesterol is found only in animal fats.) Furthermore, such claims ignored the fact that high saturated-fat content tends to increase the body's own production of cholesterol after consumption of the product. When a popular book, the *Eight Week Cholesterol Cure*, cited the benefits of oat bran in reducing blood cholesterol levels, dozens of new products and labels sprang up trumpeting the presence of oat bran, as if it were a cure-all for heart disease. Yet the scientific evidence never singled out oat bran as being any more effective than certain other forms of bran.

• *Undefined terms.* Perhaps the most common abuse in the old labeling system was the lack of legal, standard definitions for the terms used on labels. Many labels prominently displayed the word "Lite," suggesting that the products were low in fat and/or calories. But many of the items so labeled were not significantly lighter than other products. Yet it was perfectly legal to use such words even deliberately to mislead because the word "Lite" had no legally specified meaning.

• *Multiple terms for sugar.* Old labels listed ingredients in order of declining amounts present in the product. Many foods, particularly breakfast foods, were composed more of sugar than of any other single ingredient. But some companies attempted to disguise this fact by listing separately the different types of sugar—for example, sucrose, fructose, and corn syrup—each one of which was not the dominant ingredient by itself.

• *Indicating fat by weight rather than calories.* Old labels generally presented the amount of fat present by weight. For instance, if there were one gram of fat and two grams of carbohydrate in a slice of Snack Bar X, for a total of three grams, the label reported fat as 33 percent ($\frac{1}{3}$ = 33.3 percent). But health authorities say that we should be concerned with the proportion of fat calories in our diets. And since fat contains more than twice the calories of carbohydrate and protein of the same weight, Snack Bar X really contains 52.9 percent of its calories as fat! (9 calories per gram of fat divided by the total of 9 + 8—4 per gram of carbohydrate = $9/17$ = 52.9 percent.) The truth is very different from the stated claim. Similarly, whole milk contains "only" 3.2 percent of its weight in fat, but this accounts for 65 of the 150 calories (43 percent in an eight-ounce serving).

The Nutritional Labeling and Education Act of 1991

The key provisions of this law aim to solve all the problems pointed out previously regarding earlier label systems. It also calls for simplifying many other parts of the old labels. See Table 7.1 for a contrast between the old and new labels.

• *Standard serving sizes.* The Food and Drug Administration (FDA) now has standard portion sizes for over 150 different types of foods.

• *Deceptive health claims.* These are now forbidden.

• *Undefined terms.* Legal definitions are now provided for many food terms. For instance, "fat-free" means no more than 0.5 gram of fat per serving.

• *Multiple terms for sugar.* Total sugar must also be indicated.

• *The true impact of fat.* The new labels provide the number of calories provided by fat in the prod-

TABLE 7.1
FOOD LABELS THEN AND NOW

Old Style		New Style	
CHICKEN SOUP		BEEF SOUP	
Serving Size	4 oz. condensed	Serving Size	4 oz. condensed
Servings per Container	2½	Servings per Container	2½
Calories	60	Calories	180
Protein (grams)	3	Calories from fat	40
Carbohydrate (grams)	7		
Fat (grams)	2	Amount	Daily Value
Cholesterol	10 mg/serving	Fat MEDIUM (4 g)	75 g or less*
Sodium	880 mg/serving	Saturated Fat LOW (1 g)	25 g or less*
		Cholesterol LOW (4 g)	300 mg or less*
		Sodium HIGH (1,100 mg)	2,400 mg or less
Percentage of U.S. RDA		Carbohydrate LOW (25 g)	325 g or less*

Old				New	
Protein	4	Riboflavin	2	Fiber MEDIUM (3 g)	25 g
Vitamin A	8	Niacin	4	Protein MEDIUM (10 g)	None
Vitamin C	*	Calcium	*		
Thiamin	2	Iron	2	Percent of Daily Value	

		Vitamin A LOW 1	Calcium LOW 3
		Vitamin C LOW 1	Iron LOW 8

*Contains less than 2% of the
U.S. RDA of this nutrient

*As part of a 2,350-calorie diet

Ingredients: Chicken stock, enriched
macroni product, chicken meat, water,
salt, celery, modified food starch, etc.

Ingredients: Chicken stock, enriched
macaroni product, chicken meat, etc.

uct. The FDA adds a description on the label as being either "LOW," "MEDIUM," or "HIGH" to avoid making the consumer have to calculate how the product stacks up to the recommendation of 30 percent of calories or less. The new label also states the amount of saturated fat (the worst kind) and cholesterol present. These levels are also described as being low, medium, or high.

• *No more u.s. rda's.* New labels don't tell the percent of the U.S. Recommended Dietary Allowance for all nutrients. In the past, food manufacturers often listed a food's nutrients on a label no matter how little of those nutrients was actually present in the food. As a result, labels often consisted of long lists of nutrients in tiny amounts. New labels tell the "percent of daily value" only for major nutrients such as vitamin A, vitamin C, calcium, and iron—the key nutrients most likely to run short in modern diets, especially among teens. As a result, new labels are simpler and more helpful in telling how much of a major nutrient a food contains.

• *Additional information.* New labels tell you how much sodium each serving of the product contains and remind you of the recommended total "daily value" or intake. It describes the amounts of fiber, carbohydrate, and protein in terms of low, medium, and high.

The new labels may not yet be perfect, but they represent a major leap forward from the old. The new ones make understanding a product's nutritional value much easier. Could even NUTRO-MIGHT do better?

Appendix A
Source Notes

1. Jack Z. Yetiv. *Popular Nutritional Practices*. New York: Dell, 1988.

2. Bruce Ames, et al. "Dietary Pesticides (99.9% all natural)." *Proceedings of the National Academy of Sciences*. October 1990, vol. 87, p. 7777.

3. National Research Council. *Alternative Agriculture*. Washington, D.C.: National Academy of Sciences, 1989.

Appendix B
Food Organizations
to Contact
for More Information

The organizations below may be of use if you wish to learn more about specific food risks and controversies. Please note that the addresses below are accurate as of the date of publication but may change over time. The newest *Encyclopedia of Associations* in your local library can provide you the latest addresses.

Americans for Safe Food
1501 16th Street, N.W.
Washington, D.C. 20036

Environmental Protection Agency (EPA)
Office of Pesticide & Toxic Substances
Washington, D.C. 20460

Food Chemical News
1101 Pennsylvania Avenue, S.E.
Washington, D.C. 20003

Food Safety & Inspection Service
U.S. Department of Agriculture
Washington, D.C. 20250

Institute of Food Technologists
221 North LaSalle Street
Chicago, Illinois 60601

National Food Processors Association
1401 New York Avenue, N.W.
Washington, D.C. 20005

Appendix C
Further Reading

Carson, Rachel. *Silent Spring*. Boston: Houghton Mifflin, 1962.

(This book was first published in 1962. Since many of the problems it pointed out have been solved, it is mostly of historical interest now. It was the first to awaken the public to the dangers of uncontrolled pesticides.)

Reader's Digest. *Eat Better, Live Better*. Pleasantville, NY: Reader's Digest Association, 1984.

(This very readable book has interesting information on the history of food myths, the dangers of herbs and fad diets, how to detect food allergies, and many other practical topics).

Salter, Charles A. *The Vegetarian Teen*. Brookfield, CT: Millbrook, 1991.

(This book explains the health risks of various vegetarian diets and how to overcome them. It also explains the health benefits of a well-balanced vegetarian diet.)

Yetiv, Jack Z. *Popular Nutritional Practices*. New York: Dell, 1988.

(This very comprehensive book covers just about every kind of eating fad you can imagine. Some of the scientific explanations are a bit technical, but the basic issues and conclusions are presented in clear, simple language.)

Index

About the Author

Charles A. Salter is the author of three other books in Millbrook Press's Teen Nutrition Series: *Looking Good, Eating Right; The Vegetarian Teen;* and *The Nutrition-Fitness Link.* He has an undergraduate degree in psychology from Tulane University and graduate degrees in social psychology from the University of Pennsylvania and in nutrition from Harvard University. He has taught classes in nutrition at Harvard University and is a Fellow of the American College of Nutrition. In 1992 he was appointed Director of the Biomedical Applications Research Division of the U.S. Army Aeromedical Research Laboratory in Fort Rucker, Alabama.